Running head: SUPPORTING CAREGIVERS FASD

Supporting Caregivers of Children with a Fetal Alcohol Spectrum Disorder

Abstract

Parenting is an extraordinary job under the best of circumstances but becomes even more daunting when parents are attempting to parent children with a Fetal Alcohol Spectrum Disorder (FASD). Often they are parenting children that have come into their home via kinship, foster or adoptive placement. Parents may have been ill prepared to deal with the special challenges of parenting children with an FASD and the secondary disabilities that often accompany them. A majority of children with an FASD live in out of home placements and often are at high risk of placement disruption. By improving and implementing supports in the home, school and community, placements can be stabilized. Permanency is important for these children because frequent interruption in caregivers increases their risk of developing secondary disabilities and mental health disorders. Parents can find tremendous benefit from participating in a support group designed to address these unique challenges. This paper addresses the challenges of creating and sustaining a support network for parents of children with an FASD.

Table of Contents

Fetal Alcohol Spectrum Disorder Defined

According to the Fetal Alcohol Syndrome Diagnostic and Prevention network of the University of Washington, "Fetal Alcohol Spectrum Disorder (FASD) is an umbrella term describing the range of effects that can occur in an individual whose mother drank alcohol during her pregnancy. This may include physical, mental, behavioral, and/or learning disabilities with possible lifelong implications". The diagnostic term is Fetal Alcohol Syndrome (FAS) and this has been accepted as a diagnosis in the International Classification of Diseases. The American Academy of Pediatrics (2000) recognizes four different conditions resulting from maternal alcohol use during pregnancy, FAS, "...partial FAS (pFAS), Alcohol Related Birth Defects (ARBD), and Alcohol-Related Neurodevelopmental Disorder (ARND)" (as cited in Brown and Bednar, 2004, p. 2). "The overall prevalence rate of FAS and ARBD has been estimated at 10 per 1000 births" (May & Gossage, 2001 as cited in Brown and Bednar, 2004, p. 2).

FASD is a lifetime disability; the brain damage is permanent. The diagnostic criteria for an FASD are: prenatal maternal alcohol use, growth deficiency of weight/height below the 10th percentile, CNS abnormalities (structural, neurological and functional deficits) and dysmorphic features (Streissguth, 2001).

Often individuals with an FASD develop secondary disabilities due to inadequate diagnosis and services (Arendt & Farkas, 2007). Research by Streissguth (1996) has shown that other causes are disrupted school experiences, inconsistent care giving, involvement with social services and law enforcement, IQ's over 70, exposure to violence, sexual and/or physical abuse (in Kellerman, 2002).

The risks of not identifying and treating FASD are inaccurate labeling, misuse of medications, unemployment, jail, loss of family, homelessness, increased risk of substance use and premature death. The benefits of diagnosis are that diagnosis may decrease frustration and anger that others feel towards the person, increased success, improved outcomes and a decrease in future births (Arendt & Farkas, 2007).

An issue that complicates diagnosis and treatment of individuals with an FASD is that many individuals are undiagnosed (Arendt & Farkas, 2007). Often there are not physical features of a disability and the person appears quite normal. If maternal history is not known doctors may decide that children do not have an FASD because they appear normal. The lifetime economic costs of individuals with an FASD are estimated to be at $2,000,000 (Buxton, 2005).

Literature Review of Recommended Supports

The focus of research has been on education and prevention of FASD during pregnancy and identification of primary and secondary disabilities (Arendt & Farkas, 2007; Beckham, 2007; Caley, Shipkey, Winkelman, Dunlap, and Rivera, 2006; Duquette, Stodel, Fullarton, and Hagglund, 2006; Nakken, 2002; Streissguth 2001; Wedding et al., 2007). Research focus has been on prevention and treating women for alcoholism in an attempt to educate them about the dangers of consuming alcohol use during pregnancy. Despite these efforts a large number of children are still being born with alcohol related disorders. The majority of these children are being raised in out of home placements by kinship caregivers, foster parents and adoptive parents (Streissguth, 1997, 2001).

Research has shown that "12 different types of referrals are necessary" for families (Caley et al., 2006, p. 157). These referrals include service providers from education, substance abuse treatment programs, counseling agencies, FASD specialists, developmental specialists, healthcare, child protective services, and community services (Caley et al.).

Michael Dorris, an adoptive parent, wrote a book called The Broken Cord in 1989 relating his struggles to parent a child with FAS. A movie was made for television based on the book and this brought the issue of FAS into public awareness. The first book written to help families cope with the needs of children with an FASD was written by Ann Streissguth (1997) and her work has been foundational for all other research in the field. Buxton (2005) wrote a book based on her first hand experience of being a foster parent, adoptive parent and advocate for children with an FASD and she relies heavily upon previous work by Streissguth. While parent authored books are not considered to be research, the experiences of these parents have helped researchers and professionals in the field to understand the needs of families parenting children with an FASD.

Brown and Bednar (2004) have written the only article that directly addresses the challenges of parenting children with an FASD. Brown and Bednar (2004) used concept mapping as "an approach to the quantitative analysis of qualitative data" (p. 3). They advertised for parent participants who answered a telephone survey about their experiences and needs as parents of children with an FASD. The responses were analyzed and eight clusters of need were identified. The clusters were labeled as preventing setbacks, making time for parents, keeping plans, home-school collaboration, motivating child, lack of support, social isolation and behavioral problems (Brown & Bednar, 2004). Children were described as being inconsistent in their behaviors and having spotty mastery. Parents needed a break from the demands of parenting and the ability to plan for the future. Parents wanted to have a safe home environment with order and structure for the benefit of the entire family. Collaborating with educators was often a challenge because educators often did not see the entire picture. The biggest need parents had was for professionals to engage them in a team approach to caring for their child and to recognize them as an expert on their children (Brown & Bednar, 2004). Too often problems were blamed on "bad parenting" and little attempt was made to understand the families' culture or methods of parenting.

Research

Community based services

Financial Supports

Secondary Disabilities

History of previous placements

Community Attitudes

Co-occurrence of mental health diagnoses

Developmental Disabilities Services

Compassionate Care

Legislature support of agency policies

Professional Trainings

Child's age at placement

Child's Behaviors

Family Ability to Cope with Stress

Child's resiliency & ability to heal

Quality of in home services.

Child's IQ and ability to benefit from treatment

Parent viewed as an expert

Family understanding of disability

Stability of Placement

Relationship of caregivers

Respite care.

Agency Policies

Integration with peers

Insurance coverage of mental health care & residential treatment

Knowledge of Providers

Family of Origin

Support of extended family and peers.

Support of Placing Agency

Faith & Belief System

Child's School

Residential Treatment when needed

Ability of direct service providers to follow through on treatment plans

Child legal issues

Solution Focused vs. Blaming Parents

Direct Influence

Child safety and ability to keep family safe

Media portrayals of disability

Less Direct Influence

Availability of specialized care

Professional publications

Agency Budgets

Least Direct Influence

This sphere of influence shows external and internal influences on stability of placements for children with an FASD (Brown & Bednar, 2004; Buxton, 2005; Streissguth, 1997). Seeing this in a sphere of influence shows how many different factors influence placement and the potential scope of stabilizing placements. All of these factors interplay over time and will move in and out of the sphere of influence with some taking precedence over others depending on current needs of the child and family. If there is system failure in one area it is going to affect family functioning and ability to maintain stability for the child.

Internal and External Barriers to Obtaining Services for FASD

Mandell, B., & Schram, B. (2009) define internal barriers as "emotions or attitudes within a person that make it difficult for him or her to seek help" and external barriers as "environmental" (p. 14). Their definition of internal barriers can be expanded to include innate challenges that individuals may experience due to cognitive deficits caused by fetal alcohol spectrum disorders.

Human service workers frequently encounter families suffering from multiple challenges that interfere with their ability to make decisions about their lives. They may be parenting children who suffer from FASD. This situation presents unique challenges since the children have cognitive deficits and have often experienced secondary disabilities of homelessness, separation from family of origin, and mental illness (Streissguth, 1997).

The goal of case management is to "...optimize self-care capabilities of individuals and families and the capacity of systems and communities to coordinate and provide services" (Public Health Nursing Section, 2001 p. 93 as cited in Caley et al. , p. 158). Expectations have to be adjusted and the human services worker has to be competent in not just service delivery but in educating other disciplines about the unique needs of the client. Caley et al. (2006) report that research has shown that effective "...interventions have proven to prevent secondary disabilities and enhance outcomes" (p. 155).

The majority of children who have a diagnosis of an FASD are being raised in substitute care (Buxton, 2005). Buxton explains, "Among children in permanent care and thus available for adoption, 70 percent had FASD" (p. 50). Children will need help moving through the layers of grief that accompany being placed in long term care or termination of parental rights and subsequent adoption. Frequent changes of caregivers, foster and adoptive parents are not unusual when a child is being raised in state custody. Many children have experienced violence or abuse in their families of origin and while in substitute care. Education and peer relationships are interrupted by frequent moves (Arendt & Farkas, 2007). Having an IQ over seventy may make a child ineligible for special services from rural regional centers or other social services (Buxton, 2005).

Individuals with an FASD have difficulty processing information (Duquette et al., 2006). Difficulties are manifested in areas involving the taking in of information, storing information, recalling information, and using and applying what they have learned in situations. These difficulties manifest in everyday life in problem solving, applying past experiences to present situations, predicting outcomes, inability to be flexible, challenges coping with change and stress, taking things literally, feeling inadequate (different) and not wanting anyone to know. Children with an FASD can have great difficulty coping with normal environmental stresses that most of us never notice; they may have a co-occurring diagnosis of sensory integration disorder (Streissguth, 2001; Arendt and Farkas, 2007).

The primary disabilities in persons with an FASD are lower IQ, impaired ability in reading, spelling & math, lower level of adaptive functioning; more significantly impaired than IQ. Individuals perform at a lower level than you would expect them to be able to. Executive functioning is affected: the ability to take initiative, follow through on directions, concept formation, frustration tolerance, judgment, planning, problem solving, calculations and the speed of information processing (Streissguth, 2001; Arendt and Farkas, 2007).

As children move through adolescence they often develop secondary disabilities including homelessness, substance abuse, delinquency, mental health problems and unemployment. O'Malley (1999) describes these adolescents as having a "Triple Diagnosis clinical picture…a combination of organic brain dysfunction, secondary mental health problems and co-morbid addiction problems" (as cited in Buxton, 2005, p. 184). According to research done by Streissguth (1997) several factors reduce the development of secondary disabilities: a stable home environment, no exposure to violence, early diagnosis of an FASD, eligibility for developmental disabilities services and having basic needs met (as cited in Buxton, 2005; Arendt and Farkas, 2007).

Traditional approaches of mental health often fail because mental health treatment is based on the person's ability to develop insight into their behaviors, empathy for others and to follow through on treatment suggestions. Individuals with an FASD have an inability to follow through because of neurological deficits (Duquette et al., 2006; Arendt and Farkas, 2007). Treatment is expensive and outcome based. When benefits are not seen quickly then funding sources refuse to pay.

A major barrier to intervention is the lack of services. Professionals fail to recognize this as a real disability (Wedding et al., 2007). Insurance companies won't pay for treatment for behavioral problems or learning disabilities. Professionals often see FASD as behavior that the individual could gain control over or that could respond to environmental changes like better parenting and unconditional love (Brown & Bednar, 2004; Wedding et al., 2007). There is not an understanding that the behaviors observed are the result of brain dysfunction and that what is needed is to restructure how we as a society view these individuals and their families. The systems of care serving individuals with an FASD are public health, education, social services, legal and financial services.

A diagnosis of an FASD is a protective factor because it helps a child qualify for services like special education under Other Health Impaired (OHI), mental health, developmental disabilities, and early intervention services (Duquette et al., 2006). Diagnosis provides an explanation for the child's disabilities and behaviors. Becoming educated about the diagnosis helps caregivers to formulate a plan to meet the challenges of parenting the child. Diagnosis helps service providers to identify intervention strategies and to implement appropriate case management. Diagnosis helps to set up the environment for success and to minimize secondary disabilities (Arendt & Farkas, 2007).

The individual with an FASD is going to have a much harder time benefitting from any therapy designed to help them overcome living in an addictive family system and giving up their role (Nakken, 2002). Children will import the dysfunction of their family of origin into the family of substitute caregivers. Traditional interventions depend on the individual developing insight into their behavior, taking responsibility for their part in it, embracing change and abstaining from destructive patterns of behavior in the future. An individual with an FASD is often not able to delay gratification, follow through with plans agreed to in therapy or connect negative consequences with past behaviors (Beckham, 2007).

Without education and support caregivers may not understand the cognitive limitations of a child with FASD (Brown & Bednar, 2004; Arendt and Farkas, 2007). If the child identifies very strongly with the biological parents and feels that they were treated unfairly and that he was wrongfully removed from them then he will resist any attempts to get him to fit in with the new family. A child with an FASD may have a difficult time moving through the grief process and reconnecting in a new home.

It is very important that individuals with an FASD are seen as being on a continuum. There is a range of severity and not all people with the diagnosis are going to act the same way (Duquette et al., 2006). They will still have an individual personality and differ in their resiliency.

A Model for Supporting Families Caring for Children with an FASD

To address the concerns families have in caring for their children with an FASD a support group will be established. The group will meet in a meeting room at the local university.

The location has been chosen for its proximity to parking, the child care center and public transportation. A core group of parents will act as facilitators with a professor from the department for addictions acting as consultant and occasional guest speaker. The primary focus of the group will be support for parents (Caley et al., 2006; Brown & Bednar, 2004) It has been decided to make use of a twelve step model since this has been successful in other communities. Group participants will make use of the twelve steps to reflect parenting children with an FASD (Kellerman, appendix B). The state adoption unit will provide respite and group funding since they are under a federal mandate to provide funds for the support of foster and adoptive parents. Brochures will be distributed to professionals in the area. The child development center on campus has agreed to offer respite for attending parents making use of students in need of community service hours to fulfill their class requirements in special education.

The strengths parents may bring into the group are the willingness to seek services, interest in expanding knowledge, the desire to give and receive support, and a commitment to parenting the children in their care (Brown & Bednar, 2004). The challenges will be in overcoming parent frustration with the lack of community based services for their families and historical mistrust of the intentions of providers (Brown & Bednar, 2004). A major challenge the group will face is helping parents to work through their anger towards agencies for not helping enough and towards birth families for causing the child's disabilities (Buxton, 2005; Brown and Bednar, 2004). Working through the anger is part of the grieving process as they learn to embrace the child they are parenting and let go of unfulfilled parenting fantasies (Buxton, 2005). Peer support is needed because often professionals are focused on working with the child and unable to understand the need of the caregivers (Brown & Bednar, 2004).

The success of the group will depend on the ability of the group members to maintain confidentiality and safety for their membership. A twelve step model was chosen because it places responsibility for wellness directly upon each member and allows for full participation of all attendees. The twelve step model encourages members to remain involved by acting as sponsors for new attendees.

The group will be an open group available to all caregivers of children with an FASD. The group will also be open to visitors who have a desire to learn about parenting children with an FASD. In the future if confidentiality becomes a concern the group may become a closed group with newcomers and visitors seeking approval from the group before attending. Group meetings will begin with informal introductions and allow for visitors to explain their interest in attending. There is not a limitation on how many people may be involved in the group but should it become necessary in the future the group may choose to offer additional times for meetings. The limitation of adding additional times will be availability of childcare services.

The group receives necessary structure and endorsement from the university and the department for addictions with support from the childcare center and education department. Additional supports come from referring professionals (Brown & Bednar, 2004) and word of mouth from other parents. Parent involvement, state funding and donations of supplies will allow the group to function without cost. The group will depend on core membership to facilitate set up of the meeting room, preparation of refreshments, clean up and contact with the consultant and childcare center. There is not a designated leader but members may volunteer to chair meetings and take on other jobs as needed. The group will depend on the goodwill of its membership to accomplish tasks (Mandell & Schram, 2009).

The group environment will be one of respect for individuals and their journey of learning to adjust their parenting style to the needs of the children in their care. Advice giving will be discouraged in favor of listening and responding with one's own stories of overcoming difficulties. Parents have the skills they need to solve the problems they are having with the children in their care when given needed support (Brown & Bednar, 2004). Group members may form supportive relationships with each other outside of the group meetings. Time will be allowed before and after group meetings for informal visiting. Group leaders often will have an additional role outside of the group as a sponsor for newcomers. Information will be given in each meeting so that newcomers know how to reach a sponsor for further talk and encouragement.

Attendance will be the primary indicator of group efficacy. As long as interest and attendance continues core members remain committed to keeping the group active. Feedback on group attendance will be provided to the group consultant for the purpose of keeping statistics however no record will be kept of attendees for reasons of confidentiality. The exception is that parents using childcare must provide pertinent information to ensure child safety. Childcare records are to be maintained by the childcare center with all due diligence to ensure confidentiality.

The hope is that by empowering parents and providing a safe environment for the sharing of resources families will be supported and functioning will be enhanced. A natural outgrowth would be duplication of groups and expansion to surrounding communities. As parents feel empowered they will be in a better position to negotiate with service providers, educators and health care workers. Belonging to a support network will help parents overcome feelings of isolation and hopelessness. Children will benefit from time apart interacting with their peers and the educational activities provided. It would be nice to see an adolescent group started to compliment the parent group. Adolescents may also benefit by volunteering in the child care center and learning from the teachers caring for the children. The university benefits by having access to the statistics of the group and observing the model of supports for current research, funding and program planning. Students benefit by having first hand contact with children and families. Professionals will benefit by having a resource in place for referring families and as a source of information. The community will benefit from increased awareness of disabilities and the system of supports needed to help families succeed.

Conclusion

With appropriate early intervention, early diagnosis, an attempt to protect children from developing secondary disabilities and safe consistent parenting there is going to be a good chance of a positive outcome. There needs to be as much focus on the abilities as there are on the cant's. It is absolutely possible that an individual with an FASD can grow up to be a warm, caring family member and have a productive place in society. Children with an FASD have a need to be followed with lifetime services and community based care (Arendt and Farkas, 2007). This requires that society recognize FASD as a disability and not a moral failing (Buxton, 2005). Funding needs to be put in place for disability income, assisted living, homemaker services, and vocational training. Additionally resources need to be expanded in education, public health and awareness of the permanent disabilities caused by alcohol use during pregnancy. (Buxton, 2005). While much is known about FASD, there still remains a need to support families and to receive full recognition as a disability. When families feel supported they have the best chance of achieving success. Implementation of support groups for families will lead to advocacy and better understanding of the needs of individuals with an FASD. As public awareness and acceptance increases it is expected that funding of services will increase and that outcomes will improve.

References

Arendt, R., & Farkas, K. (2007). Maternal alcohol abuse and fetal alcohol spectrum disorder: A life-span perspective. *Alcoholism Treatment Quarterly, 25*(3), 3-20. doi:10.1300/j020v25n03_02 Retrieved on 05/12/2009, from Liberty University Web site: http://www.EBSCOHost.org

Beckham, N. (2007). Motivational interviewing with hazardous drinkers. *American Academy of Nurse Practitioners, 19,* 103-110. Retrieved on 05/12/2009, from Liberty University Web site: http://www.EBSCOHost.org

Brown, J., & Bednar, L. (2004). Challenges of parenting children with a fetal alcohol spectrum disorder: A concept map. *Journal of Family Social Work, 8*(3), 1-18. doi:http://www.haworthpress.com/web/JFSW Retrieved on 05/12/2009, from Liberty University Web site: http://www.EBSCOHost.org

Buxton, B., (2005). *Damaged angels: An adoptive mother discovers the tragic toll of alcohol in pregnancy.* New York, NY: Carroll & Graf Publishers

Caley, L., Shipkey, N., Winkelman, T., Dunlap, C., & Rivera, S. (2006). *Evidence-based review of nursing interventions to prevent secondary disabilities in fetal alcohol spectrum disorder. Pediatric Nursing, 32*(2), 155-162. Retrieved on 05/12/2009, from Liberty University Web site: http://www.EBSCOHost.org

Fetal Alcohol Syndrome Diagnostic and Prevention Network, University of Washington: Seattle, WA http://depts.washington.edu/fasdpn/htmls/research.htm

Duquette, C., Stodel, E., Fullarton, S., & Hagglund, K. (2006). Teaching students with developmental disabilities. *Teaching: Exceptional Children, 39*(2), 28-31. Retrieved on 05/12/2009, from Liberty University Web site: http://www.EBSCOHost.org

Mandell, B., & Schram, B. (2009). *Introduction to human services: Policy and practice* (7th ed.). Boston, MA: Pearson Education, Inc.

Nakken, J. (2002). Reflections on the past, present and possible future of women's alcoholism treatment. *Alcoholism Treatment Quarterly, 20*(3/4), 147-156. Retrieved on 05/12/2009, from Liberty University Web site: http://www.EBSCOHost.org

Streissguth, A.P., Barr, H.M., Kogan, J. & Bookstein, F. L., (1996). *Understanding the Occurrence of Secondary Disabilities in Clients with Fetal Alcohol Syndrome (FAS) and Fetal Alcohol Effects (FAE),* Final Report to the Centers for Disease Control and Prevention (CDC), August, 1996, Seattle: University of Washington, Fetal Alcohol & Drug Unit, Tech. Rep. No. 96-06, (1996) in Kellerman 2000-2002, retrieved on 05/11/09 from www.come-over.to/FAS/fasconf.htm

Streissguth, A. (1997). *Fetal alcohol syndrome: A guide for families and communities.* Baltimore, MD: Paul H. Brooks Publishing.

Streissguth, A. (2001). Recent advances in fetal alcohol syndrome and alcohol use in pregnancy. In D.P. Agarwal (Ed.), *Alcohol in Health and Disease* (pp. 303-324). New York, NY: Marcel Dekker, Inc.

Wedding, D., Mengel, M., Ulion, M., Cook, K., Kohout, J., Ohlemiller, M., et al. (2007). Psychologists' knowledge and attitudes about fetal alcohol syndrome, fetal alcohol spectrum disorders, and alcohol use during pregnancy. *Professional Psychology: Research and Practice, 38*(2), 208-213. doi:10.1037/0735-7028.38.2.208 Retrieved on 05/12/2009, from Liberty University Web site: http://www.EBSCOHost.org

Appendix A

Interview with a Caregiver

1. *Please briefly describe your child.*

   Matthew is a seventeen year old male who came into foster care in our home with a plan of adoption in March 1997.

2. *Please describe your child's history.*

   Matthew came into our care with the diagnosis of Fetal Alcohol Syndrome (FAS), Fetal Drug Effect (FDE), Post Traumatic Stress Disorder (PTSD), Reactive Attachment Disorder (RAD), Attention Deficit Hyperactive Disorder (ADHD) and Oppositional Defiant Disorder (ODD). There is family history of bi-polar and borderline personality disorder on the maternal side. Mom was known to local Division of Child and Family Services (DCFS) since she had been in and out of care throughout her childhood. Mom had a history of alcohol use and poly drug use with cocaine being her drug of choice. Less is known of dad's history although he also grew up in care and had a significant history of substance use and domestic violence. Matthew came into care with a younger and older sibling. A fourth sibling was born after mom & dad had signed voluntary termination of parental rights (TPR). TPR was pursued after failed attempts at reunification with mom & dad. The children were placed in two previous adoptive homes and DCFS was asked to move the children when the potential parents became overwhelmed by the children's extensive needs.

3. *What is your relationship to Matthew?*

   I am Matthew's adoptive father. I am also the adoptive parent of two of his siblings.

4. *What were your impressions of the child upon placement?*

The most significant thing I noticed about Matthew soon after placement was his rage. He seemed filled with a rage that did not seem characteristic or appropriate for a child his age. He acted out by hitting and tormenting his siblings.   When asked to do simple tasks or corrected he would fly into a rage and pull things off shelves, kick the furniture and in other ways destroy whichever room he happened to be in.   When restrained he would attempt to head butt, bite, pull hair and spit. His tantrums were long lasting and seemed out of proportion for what had happened. The developmental specialist had described him as severely emotionally disturbed in her initial report and I found that to be true. He was confused about who his family was and seemed very upset to have been removed from a previous adoptive home however he did not make any mention of his biological family. He could be best described as a child with a chip on his shoulder. At other times he was quite sunny and cuddly. He seemed very eager to have a daddy and to do things together. He loved coming outside to help with chores or to go on outings to fish or camp. In many ways it seemed that it would be as the social worker promised; that he simply needed unconditional love and a secure home environment and then he would make a good recovery from his past traumas. Over the years he would continue to have frequent problems in school, with neighborhood kids and at home. I would be asked to remove him from Sunday school, Scouts and other activities because of inappropriate and disruptive behaviors.

5.   *Were there professionals who were helpful to you?*

We were quite fortunate to work with a knowledgeable child psychiatrist until he took a teaching position at Brown University. It was during this time that I was coming to realize that Matthew was not going to outgrow his problems. We tried different medications to control his behaviors with minimal results.   We also saw a Christian psychologist for several years for therapy.   As much as we loved Dr. Bob it never seemed like Matthew was making

any progress. A large focus of therapy was in giving me support and helping me to cope

with his behaviors. I also felt a need to have all behaviors documented because of concerns

of false allegations of abuse by Matthew and his siblings. Lying and stealing were frequent

concerns to the point of not being able to take Matthew into stores. There were also incidents

of stealing at school and in the homes of friends. Our pediatrician has also been very

supportive over the years. She has felt the burden of trying to manage his care when

insurance has been reluctant to pay for mental health services. Seen less frequently were the

dentist, orthodontist & eye doctor. While she was still here we saw the developmental

specialist but once she moved to Tucson we only flew to see her once.   We also saw a

neuropsychologist once in Tucson for evaluation. I always felt the doctors were doing all

they could but in the end it seemed there was nothing they could do except to document a

case history. At age thirteen Matthew's behaviors had become more extreme and out of

control putting his safety and the safety of the other children at risk. At that time he was

already involved with juvenile probation and fearing incarceration we admitted him to a

residential treatment facility.

6.   What community based services have you received?

Initially we dealt with DCFS but once the adoption was finalized they stopped services.

Actually all services stopped about nine months before his adoption. He was placed with us

in March of 1997 and by August they felt he was stable enough to move to a lower level of

care so they offered to move him or leave him with us if we would give up our affiliation

with XYZ Foster Homes (a Christian based provider of contracted social services) and

become a level one foster home.   Since we wanted to adopt the children we agreed to part ways with XYZ. This was a huge mistake because we immediately lost their support and services. At that time we were not skilled enough to know that we could have had him evaluated and certified to continue with therapeutic care. We thought since DCFS said he was fine that there was no need for specialized services. We had been receiving services at Children's Behavioral Services but once the adoption was completed they asked us to begin paying for services. Again we didn't know that they needed to pursue Medicaid as a pay source. We also didn't know we could be reimbursed for transportation. It all sounds so naïve now, but at the time we really didn't know these things and since we couldn't afford the co-pays and to continue the travel we quit going. Since Matthew was determined not to need specialized care by DCFS we did not qualify for a large adoption subsidy. Our income did not allow us to qualify for state services so we were in a bind. My wife had given up county employment to be a full time mother to the children. There were so many red flags in the adoption process that we didn't see at the time and we were so eager to adopt and help Matthew that we were blinded to his disabilities and what his long term needs would be. He had been eligible for an Individual Education Plan (IEP) under Developmentally Delayed (DD) until he went to kindergarten. At that time he did not test poorly and we were told that he was no longer eligible for services. We were told that he needed to show a 50% delay in order to qualify for special education. Again we did not know any better and accepted what the school district told us. It was only after some years of really struggling that we came to understand how the IEP process worked and insisted on an evaluation for special education for Other Health Impaired (OHI). The school psychologist was very reluctant but conducted the testing and would only agree to have a 504 put in place. Matthew never received any special education services at all. In sixth grade he was suspended for bringing a utility knife to school. His behavior was deteriorating and he was not succeeding in sports or academics.

He became involved with juvenile probation prevention services. By seventh grade he was in danger of being placed on formal probation. By the time he was discharged from residential treatment into a group home his stated goal for his life was to pursue a lifestyle of criminal activity. He was placed on juvenile parole and remanded to a youth training center at age fourteen. He was released to a group home only to be remanded again a short time later again to a youth training center for possession of a stolen vehicle and guns. He had multiple stays in juvenile detention centers and two short stays at home prior to this. He was discharged into a residential training program and is currently residing in a group home with plans to transition to independent living at age eighteen in a few months. He has not completed high school and has been unable to find a job. As his behavior presents a risk to the safety of the other children in my home he is not able to return here to live. As long as he remains on parole they may continue to offer him services until age nineteen or transfer his case to the adult parole division. As he has not benefitted from treatment and there is a lack of funding it is most likely he will be remanded as an adult.

7. *What successes have you seen with this child?*

Unfortunately I have seen few successes. Matthew is at about a third grade level academically.   Therapists tell us his emotional functioning is at the level of a first grader. Matthew has significant impairment of his functional abilities; he does not seem able to take care of himself or to live outside of a highly structured environment. By the time we knew how to advocate for him it seemed too little too late. We also found that we were limited by our own insurance, Medicaid and other resources. We have to redefine success to mean he was kept safe in school for six years. For six years we were able to keep him in a stable home and school with people who cared about him. For six years we were able to protect him from abuse and violence. For six years we were able to pursue therapy and health care. We were able to expose him to typical family life and a faith that we felt was important and consistent with that of his biological family.   For six years we were able to slow down the train wreck but we couldn't stop it. There lies a sense of failure, guilt and shame. How could we have been so naïve and how could the system fight so hard against us to keep him from getting services? We wanted so badly to give this boy a good life but we couldn't do it alone. We needed collaboration from the school district and social services and we didn't know how to make that happen.

8. *What has been your greatest challenge?*

The greatest challenge has been getting up each day and trying again and again without seeing evidence of change. Having agencies and professionals often see us as the source of the problem and blaming poor parenting for the behaviors of the child. Before the adoption we were considered to be excellent parents. Being told that he seemed just fine and they couldn't see a problem so therefore they couldn't treat it or offer services. The feeling of isolation that comes from not being able to connect with anyone who understands the daily challenges of raising a child who appears normal, but is in fact disabled. Not being believed even when we had a diagnosis. Deeper than that is the unfulfilled longings we had to be parents and to have a family and despite all of our efforts those dreams remain empty. To look at family photos and that child is not in the picture because they are in residential treatment or incarcerated. To face holidays and know that child will not be at the table. To dread grandchildren who may be as impaired as the parent. Even worse to dread grandchildren because of the certain fear that they will be abused and we feel powerless to prevent it. Knowing that we have imported dysfunction into our marriage and family and to see how it has hurt other family members when that was never our intention. We sought to create a family with joy and happiness and instead we became trapped in a nightmare.

9. *What support has been available to you from the community?*

There is little support for parents whose children deviate from the norm, even less so for parents who knowingly adopted and brought alcohol affected children into their homes. When you give birth everyone rejoices with you but when the older child is adopted it often goes un-noticed by the community. There is a pervasive belief by the community and professionals that love conquers all and if you have failed then you just didn't love enough. My wife is my greatest support.

10. *How has this changed your view of foster care and adoption?*

This may not be popular but I am totally against adoption. I feel deceived by DCFS, robbed of my youth. I feel like they shoved this child into my home and ran in the other direction. They knew they were setting us up to fail and they did nothing to prevent it. It is criminal that they can destroy families and not be held accountable for their actions. DCFS did not educate us regarding the child's history, disability or future needs. They did not put the support services in place that might have helped him to succeed. We can never recover the years we have lost in parenting this child. Years that should have been invested in our own family, saving for retirement and creating a future together. We instead live in fear that he will be released and harm us or that he will make an ally who will help him carry out the same. We are afraid for our safety and we do not feel safe in our own home. Our reputation in the community has been tarnished and that is not something we can recover. When we adopted we had plenty of friends who wrote glowing recommendations and a clean record with DCFS. That is no longer true. Even though we have never been charged nor had a founded allegation against us we have a history with DCFS that we feel can put our other children and future employment at risk. I am not sure that our family will ever fully recover from the trauma that has occurred because of our taking in children that we desperately wanted to help but failed so miserably with. In contrast I feel that the biological parents were allowed to

shirk responsibility for their children. I believe more should have been done to keep the

children in the home and to hold the parents accountable for raising their own children.

Appendix B
Twelve Steps of Fetal Alcohol Spectrum Disorders
based on the 12 Steps of AA
© 2003 Teresa Kellerman

1. We admitted we were powerless over the nature of FASD; that our lives had become unmanageable.

2. Came to believe that the power of factual information, raised awareness, mutual support, and realistic expectations could restore us to sanity.

3. Made a decision to turn our problems and concerns over to the support group.

4. Made a searching and fearless moral inventory of FASD issues in our life.

5. Admitted to ourselves and others the exact nature of our mistakes.

6. Were entirely ready to let go of past regrets and mistakes and to face the reality of FASD.

7. Humbly asked the support group to help us overcome our shortcomings.

8. Made a list of all persons in our life that FASD has affected, and became willing to educate them about FASD.

9. Shared relevant information with such people to raise their level of awareness wherever possible, except when to do so would injure them or others.

10. Continued to take personal inventory and when FASD issues crop up to promptly share with the group.

11. Sought through listening and sharing to improve our active participation with the group, asking for knowledge of effective intervention and prevention strategies and the power to carry that out.

12. Having had a personal awakening as the result of these steps, we tried to carry this message to other families, professionals and providers, and to practice these principles in all our affairs.

Made in the USA
San Bernardino, CA
30 September 2015